W9-CFJ-577

SandCastle

What Should I Eat?

Milk is Magnificent

Amanda Rondeau

Consulting Editor
Monica Marx, M.A./Reading Specialist

ABDO
Publishing Company

Published by SandCastle™, an imprint of ABDO Publishing Company, 4940 Viking Drive, Edina, Minnesota 55435.

Printed in the United States.

Credits
Edited by: Pam Price
Curriculum Coordinator: Nancy Tuminelly
Cover and Interior Design and Production: Mighty Media
Photo Credits: Brand X Pictures, Comstock, Corbis Images, Corel, Eyewire Images, PhotoDisc

Library of Congress Cataloging-in-Publication Data

Rondeau, Amanda, 1974-
    Milk is magnificentl / Amanda Rondeau.
      p. cm. -- (What should I eat?)
    Summary: A simple introduction to the milk or dairy group of foods and why those foods are important for us to eat.
    ISBN 1-57765-837-X
    1. Dairy products--Juvenile literature. 2. Nutrition--Juvenile literature. [1. Dairy products. 2. Nutrition.] I. Title.

TX556.M5 R66 2002
641.3'7--dc21

                    2002018363

SandCastle™ books are created by a professional team of educators, reading specialists, and content developers around five essential components that include phonemic awareness, phonics, vocabulary, text comprehension, and fluency. All books are written, reviewed, and leveled for guided reading, early intervention reading, and Accelerated Reader® programs and designed for use in shared, guided, and independent reading and writing activities to support a balanced approach to literacy instruction.

Let Us Know

After reading the book, SandCastle would like you to tell us your stories about reading. What is your favorite page? Was there something hard that you needed help with? Share the ups and downs of learning to read. We want to hear from you! To get posted on the ABDO Publishing Company Web site, send us email at:

sandcastle@abdopub.com

SandCastle Level: Transitional

What is the milk group?

*For suggested serving sizes, see page 22.

This is the food pyramid.

There are 6 food groups in the pyramid.

The food pyramid helps us know how to eat right.

Eating right helps us stay healthy.

The milk group is part of the food pyramid.

We should eat 2 to 3 servings from the milk group every day.

The milk group is good for our bodies.

There are many kinds of foods in the milk group.

One kind is the cheese we put on pizza.

Milk gives us vitamins that we need.

Foods in the milk group make our bones and teeth strong.

Did you know ice cream is in the milk group?

Ice cream comes in many flavors, like chocolate, mint, or strawberry.

Ice cream is a fun treat to eat!

Did you know yogurt is in the milk group?

Yogurt can be made from the milk of sheep, goats, or cows.

Yogurt is good for making smoothies.

Did you know cheese is in the milk group?

Cheese can be white, yellow, orange, or even blue!

Cheese is great for a snack or on sandwiches or pizza.

Did you know that cows have four stomachs?

Cows make most of the milk we drink.

Milk is great to drink with meals.

Can you think of other foods in the milk group?

What is your favorite food in the milk group?

Index

What Counts As a Serving?

Milk, Yogurt, and Cheese		
1 cup of milk or yogurt	1½ ounces of natural cheese	2 ounces of process cheese

Glossary

bone   the hard tissues that form a skeleton

serving   a single portion of food

smoothie   a drink usually made with yogurt and fruit blended together

teeth   the hard, white parts of the mouth that are used for chewing and biting

treat   something special

vitamin   a substance that we need for good health, found naturally in meats and plants

yogurt   a food made with curdled milk and active cultures

About SandCastle™

A professional team of educators, reading specialists, and content developers created the SandCastle™ series to support young readers as they develop reading skills and strategies and increase their general knowledge. The SandCastle™ series has four levels that correspond to early literacy development in young children. The levels are provided to help teachers and parents select the appropriate books for young readers.

Emerging Readers
(no flags)

Beginning Readers
(1 flag)

Transitional Readers
(2 flags)

Fluent Readers
(3 flags)

These levels are meant only as a guide. All levels are subject to change.

ABDO
Publishing Company

To see a complete list of SandCastle™ books and other nonfiction titles from ABDO Publishing Company, visit www.abdopub.com or contact us at:

4940 Viking Drive, Edina, Minnesota 55435 • 1-800-800-1312 • fax: 1-952-831-1632